The Corybantes

a book of Strophaics

Tod Thilleman

with an afterword by Matthew Seidman

spuyten duyvil

1997

Cover design and layout by One World Solutions.
Cover photograph of Kate Stoddard at Fire Island
courtesy of Pat & Satch Stoddard.

Some of these strophes first appeared, in a different
arrangement, in *Antenym*, edited by Steve Carll.

Spuyten Duyvil
PO Box 1852
Cathedral Station
New York, NY 10025
212-978-3353
fax: 212-727-8228

Library of Congress Cataloging-in-Publication Data

Thilleman, Tod.
        The Corybantes / Tod Thilleman
                p.   cm.
        ISBN 1-881471-18-7 (hdc.).   ISBN 1-881471-19-5 (pbk.)
        I. Title.
PS3570.H453C67   1997
811'.54--dc21   97-707
                                                   CIP

For Katya

all
out along the bias

The Corybantes

The Master Architect has arranged horizons in a renewing design.

• Robert Duncan •
"Stimmung"

In the ordinary interpretation, the stream of time is defined as *irreversible* succession. Why cannot time be reversed? Especially if one looks exclusively at the stream of "nows," it is incomprehensible in itself why this sequence should not present itself in the reverse direction. The impossibility of this reversal has its basis in the way public time originates in temporality, the temporalizing of which is primarily futural and "goes" to its end ecstatically in such a way that it "is" already towards its end.

—Martin Heidegger
Being and Time

Chorus of Spirits
And our singing shall build
In the void's loose field
A world for the Spirit of Wisdom to wield;
We will take our plan
From the new world of man,
And our work shall be called the Promethean.

—Percy Bysshe Shelley
Prometheus Unbound

For I've flicked up all the crambs as they crumbed from your table um, singing glory allaloserem, cog it out, here goes a sum. So read we in must book. It tells. He prophets most who bilks the best.

—James Joyce
Finnegans Wake

The weak must get along with nothing—or—burn in the open and set fire to the world!

—Lorine Niedecker
Letter to Zukofsky

Ontology, what is it
but that resides in being
yet threatens to erase it
How would one dare
confuse with the vast earth
self-becoming sloth man did
now pays and is bled
losing final time in midst of being
Not only would lack of speech
end this progression, all would
be forced admit mind in snare of talk

I don't quite see
why I'm so upset with everyone
existence is such an interminable joke
　　Terrible feeling of incompleteness
an alarm, the water almost capsizing
then no more fear
　　The tragedy of consumption
directive utility
haranguing identity with time
remakes land in a foolscape
　　That a praxis exists
does not still the young science
into one mode's interpretation over another
　　Death and corruption
are not the feet of balance
being should walk upon
　　Ponderous being, something forgotten
unbearable burden becomes
a release resting in things
　　The ocean and its weather
destroys beach-side real estate

Mankind
is love, and beyond that
will he rule to measure
as the ocean continues
against land
    The earth, my home
is as far from me
as the forest in the middle of my book
    Corybantic
contention with the Earth-Wave
    That's all it ever is or was
speaking to the distance
a conflagration turned substance
and hence brought near
    Presence evolves
absence is being
without becoming
she appeared, I stared
benumbed and entranced
    Systems of understanding
present weapons-at-hand

which contanment containment
being suffers at the behest of
      I do have a methodology
through the practical employment
of the value of my fetishism and models
      Light as seafoam
there's your verse
      Scoundrels and ultimately worthless
all those who can't admit to being jolted
through and through
by a woman either clothed or naked
      I am not interested
in the mechanisms that create meaning
but of what else, not spells
though THEY, ultimately, command attention
      Surprised
to find my imprint at the beach
still in place, I could have sat
all night there and the tide never would've
reached
      To hear being discourse

is not often gotten
not exclusively gotten
through speech
        We went from a mesh-fetish
from a model whose being
was constantly in question
and therefore substituted easily
to a mesh strophe
thence easily to a mosaic
which now must remain where it is
and await some final "decision"
        Time brings with it
pleasure's increase that time had diminished
        Ah the shame of it all!
(shame as a possible factoid)
        Poets will endeavor
to justify their ambiguities
the same way society justifies its modes of gossip
as what is indeed happening
whether science proves a radically
disagreeing ontology

Are you reading my mind
all you waves
    Man's worth so seldom winkled
yet his being's might
science sucks
    You must be with the herd
no one honors cultivated silence
but they covet, and then condemn
    The question is
which have we decided
to reside in, land or sea
    Over all else yet I must
come drip from aporia's tide-crest
forest's fenced-in fester
announcing daylight above to grab
a branch between, tooth and tongue
slavering energetic camouflage
appearance of the absolute
    Place drags against
pulls faster than will
tosses me up disguised order

understood as their own
     The clinking closet latch
in the bedroom as I walk past
     Man is shunted from growth
by the preponderance of being
so small is he as Venus
subdues the very sea
     In being
there is knowledge
the which's water
one day to flood ashore
     If sex isn't THE controlling wave
I wouldn't be
     Psychology, because of
and solely because of its terminal poles
creates a rigid determinism
by which to measure and infiltrate
all else
     A possible theme a possible reason
shot through me
     Have tried to keep forward

as if to encounter synthesis?
tho it doesn't matter, no one immediate
to witness nor to judge
   Objectivism
has done much damage
in that it (unknowingly)
constructs a methodology
without defining being's trace
and poses an 'as if'
in the place of concern
that is, being
(it is 'as if'
the world had already fallen into the ocean)
   Nothing but condescending
fools full of heartache
histrionic advice of lunacy
poured over my poetry, my life
   That that stands out
looks out of place, is the outcast
given sufficient time to be
to become, begins to make sense

What consumed
most of an animal's life in constructing
so too most of man's time's spent
hustling, pimping, concocting seduction
        By everything we do know
we'll know more of the mystery
never exhausted but by explication
diaphragm's dissolving mesh
        Looks like someone's in the bedroom
curtain's shadow moves
crossing wall eclipsing light
        Psychology attempts to find
manifestation of authorship
everywhere
        As for myself
and maybe for others
man simply does not interest
as a course of study
though I remain
        The individual is a weed
and a good common green

will have none of them
        Nature
in its very necessary growth
toward decon-animation
shows us the concealment
by which mankind has been baffled
confused, and just plain vengeful
raising his conscience to the status of being
before becoming
        And yet
doesn't the impulse to stop
mad gains of man's propriety
support itself on the whim
unconscious urge
humanity's fait accompli?
        The clinamen of mind
to forget and assume itself
not in eyes but absence, mystery
        Now, because of the changing tide
wave leaps higher
        Such an immediate collapse

that wave had no tube-roll
    These cupped ways of knowing
which secure belief and stave off anxiety
do not belong in books
books should BE in the world
books, primarily, should not attempt
a theatricality of understanding
but rather BE in the world
a shape not recognizable as presence
nor its negation in absence
but discover what shore-erosion
being itself accomplishes
    Fatigue's no excuse
must plunge into the organic
show its shape as it dies
    One has to ask
how is science
able to do what all it does
    The ocean worries the shore
breaking dunes in a moment by moment
image of its own collapsing self

People want to be worked up
but flee as if it were heinous to do so
          The possibility
that it could be you
remains the effort of your time
sole duty of the gift of self-identity
          Zukofsky, however
because of his love for Spinoza
no doubt, saves objectivist aesthetic
by proclaiming that a poet
writes one poem his whole life long
          It is not so much the strophaic
mosaic assemblage, nor the letters
that go to make up word
but book elicits anxiety
in the strongholds of idle talk
of rumor and the fetishism's ontology
          Any of this germane
to the book at hand?
          With the gellid
round fish dissolved

man rises on haunches
to carry out his code
     As if to call the instruments
to attention before the music to be played
a large green wave, fat
and imposing, rises and stalks the surf
     Most women have a latent fear of men
got from the touch of a man's being's direction
and since it cannot be denied or derailed
they fantasize a violence emanating from it
as if IT were any different than the extension
by which they themselves mask knowledge
the human animal in the throes of ideation
which evolves slowly, subtly
in humankind's daily existentials
     Under tree's shadow
from out of sun
     The rhythm of all these ideas
is the only lasting ideation
because the most accessible by the many
     What construct, concept

or sense
not touched by being and so
of necessity redefined
  Why is your being
always more important than mine
is this some tragic character flaw?
  The fact that these poems
are a book
make each ideogrammic stanza's sense
  The hand of becoming
reaching out to the farness of being
clears the senses and sanitizes the soul
  When there is a system
in the fall of civilization
in effect and raised with much force
disastrous are the consequences
terror the game
  I'm talking too much
trying to see what looks like
  But wait! the people gather
raise loud cries with weapons brandishing

to hunt out tyranny to its root!
      As soon as I walk in the house
I'm yakking up a storm
      Drinking buckets of ontological potion
mankind is continually in process of being drugged
      Tired
the warm but strong seawind
easily pushing my eyelids closed
      A stalk of wood on a wave-wrecked beach
flat and sharded in the noon-day sun
      All this sea-verse is pregnant
maybe with little bubbles
housing crustaceans I saw the little birds eat
      We put too much emphasis
on judgement
as the key to unlocking doors
      At the incipient collapse of Knossos
Corybantes sang in the grove on that island
Rhea's minion's raised for revolution
mankind awaited
a bull from the sea

   The objection to a foreign tongue
entered into an english work
rests on the assumption that the break
in breath and therefore rhythm
causes the scansion and begs the feet
full-stop, though the english begs continue
   There is no other mode
but the one that insists
to happen now
   This whole enterprise is sexual
which basis will be laid at the poet's feet
he has been given only to fuck
hence consumed by being
   You might as well take all the people
sweep them away and replace with a rock
the point of your discourse in the ensuing void
would stay the same
though soon you'd tire
of incessant masturbation
   I think I'm falling in love
with my notebook

Not only do I see the promised land
marching out from the waves of lettered script
but banks and other also less knowledgeable
keepers of the prime
    Early morning sun with
a bird and a cricket
and a creaking tree trunk
    Small top of a wave
splashes out a salute
before diving
    All poetry is contemporary
in that it attempted to write the historicity
of things and phenomena
within the element of individuality
    The spell has no method
but its success depends upon
a balance with nature
thus seducing realisms
    The world is balanced
by the feeding frenzy of lions
their cubs, mates, and families

      Can't hold on
to metabolism
wind increasing out of the south
      Nothing more exhilarating
pleasurable and satisfying
than when fiction overturns truth
      How much more gum-flap
when the slot's rhythm's already proposed
we all go, in fact
birth not withstanding
      My age
succumbs to rigid behaviorism
not unlike any other
      Now those footprints
emerging from where the tide was
engage my mind
      That nut-hatch
made a nest in the tree that grows from the deck
the same way being cast its spell upon the world
      Man's moods
are so uninviting for study

we'd rather wait this world out
patience, now become a centerpiece
where trivial worlds collide
and scatter themselves on the wind
      Close and nerve-rending
then to come back from afar
the round depth of sound's words
      Fact: the farthest from here
is the forest
      At the crossroads of the contradiction
nature/man, appears difference
self whose grave being announces
      Sleep's the great master
of our day as surely as our night
      The profound touch of chaos
the shell of the world
slowly informing space travel
with its feedback
      Now fetish gives way to mosaic
as sea to land and model stills
ontology the bone of contention

Take this blind from me
hate and love's hard core
sentient what seen and become
water's contanment refused
accepted, and sent
      Cloaked in time
anything can become
the fabric of behavior
      How much force, what measure
makes the ocean sound
like a jet engine
      What does it matter the reason
when industry establishes
utile and the inutile
      To enter into being through existence
enter into man through becoming being's
many-faceted sometimes strange bed cover
      To release and release
these are the waves that know me
for which, in hell
my prick the people demand

be made to stay consubstantially erect
and ready for penetration
      The house
like an artificial hymen
prophylactic engendering psychosis monumental
      I will gather in my limbs
and plant modesty
in the waters of hell
      A deer was just up on the deck
      I'm telling you
christians better get their act together
or they are swamped
      Now
the Corybantes are still ecstatically singing
but as a group (with maybe some stragglers)
they approach the shore's waves
and become one with its commotion
      A thing is still a thing
no matter the width the narrative bridge
identity continually proposes
      My acquaintances

are so rigidly determined
to cut off their heads
bodies would still find a habit to perform
      All what I've to do
be in its presence
never sure who, being
becoming nor what time
but the time of man
      I speak to you, as always
through crowning quantity of popular hearing
fine distinction left for intimacy only
sexual rumor our friendship engenders
      Tender rumors of feeling
parables of human kindness
fiction, fomalhaut of the southern fish
      Nothing in the world
has ever been concerned
with signification
except dundering fools
whose business it is
to produce such ersatz tools

I'm concerned
with finding life in literature
others are concerned with life elsewhere
     What so long fought
within a single curving wave
collapses
     Mangy cat-bird
crying in the bushes
     Latent, in the knowledge of being
there comes to form
a reflexive philosophy
whose instinct resides in the possible disguise
or undisguised it gave birth to
whose return will not occur
though anticipation in the outside world
works it to repeat, to be reborn
individuality is distinctive
and will with time be lost
in the world, and take up
new and here-to-fore alien modes
     To take a vacation

I would wish this island well
absorbed into its womb of rest
a being whose science's poetry
needs great gusts of sea air
  Eyes and ears
not the underlings of fashion
man has lived long and continues
whether put away in stone
or the foundries of metallic glee
  I'm putting it on rail, man
no backside, man
no clonker on a shoot-out
it's just not sick enough, man
  The names are sucking my purpose
urging me to return, re-examine
re-think the whole enterprise
  Wealth tends to create
an artificial closeness
the nature of being does not possess
  For all the lazy iniquity of man
I scribbled a note

A hundred white ripples
before my foot as I kick
      That man may know himself
ends nothing but search for knowledge
why we're so built, as much to ask
why the Ibis flies
      The fiction that words engender
satisfies deeply
      Without the sea
science would dry up
and beat itself to death
      All this error
the pine tree
still grows through deck
slatterned round the house
      This way
presence is/was never more than
mother's tit
      People will keep you away
from the anxiety your possible death
must bring about

they as much as do the same
to themselves by ignoring and dismissing
their reflection in the mirror
     My book needs, and is demanding
a methodology?
     Man issued a gag order
and put the whammy
on his evolution
     Shove your organic cooking
give me something to eat
     When I see a text
I WANT to read it
     150 years later
and lame anti-transcendentalists
still screaming about their "community"
as if that's going to change the always
prevailing conjugations of cowardice
     Man did not begin
appearance to his face
but far and away
the encumbrance of biologic apodictics did

Mosaic is not a methodology
Man seems not to know
language encumbers being
therefore impeding itself
Eventually
being will tire of being told
it has to work to make everything fit
and will seek to acquire, just then
the world entire
Bird ticking in the night bushes
I imagine to be the size of a human
taking up more space than its species would
and from this, a sudden threat
Mounting that body
sticking in pleasure
guiding with influence
must be mastered
To break nature down
show how it works
satisfies an innate need in man
to express himself

I want to break
let go all this head's torsion
into the camouflage of nature
unknown as any beast
        Some people spend money
on such places as this island
buying property away from the people
not to study the flat planes
the aesthetics of the place, but to come back
as it were, to a place of primal release
        The problem is
if you say anything
the behavior of the populace
grips you with scandal and feces
        It is very dangerous
when anti-matter attaches to your being
because it thinks everything is matter
precluding existence
        There is no metaphoric analogy
when all affairs are sexual
        I have nothing but my being

in excelsis
to push through people's windows
    Labor and masturbation
repetitive substitutives
energy leaving energy gaining exercises
    That camouflage threw up the virulent earth
I wrestled with, now composes
my manhood entire
    Who cares
what I think, or what I actuate
    I'm going to land and sea's
connexion
    Reason stakes a claim on being
demanding it be allowed to complete itself
    What has come about
in the writing of waves
as the material availability
for the expression of the passage (human)
to sight
    The camouflage or mask of literary adventure
finds its source in nature

but its pen is soon outdone
in a final flirtation with science
      Clean colored water
glass-clear, perfect
      Night is so peaceful and pleasant
out here alone
      In the cupped matter
in the cupped hands bring forth
inestimable spells
      Looking all around at the horizon
blue and telephone poles and houses
      Signs of behavior
trigger further behavior
      The organic structure of the world
is the structure of being
thereof the mind is swayed
      A little bell
or buckle of metal chimes
      Burning resentment
for any limitation put upon
      No one

went to work to save my being
because everyone
went to work to save my being
    Poets are not involved
with the theatricality of reason
but with the breath
of reason
obviously, no use for this
and hence no money, maybe
a trickle
    Our democracy our america
with all of its attendant belief
revolutionary or reactionary
is a real estate
    I hear
the feeding frenzy for economization
of the presentation of being
commence
    I absolutely crawl
out of my skin when I see a pretty girl
    Access to the mosaic

granted after and only after
the seeming onanism of ontology
    First and foremost
there's a decision to be made
did a bull leap from the sea?
    All the white foam
the wind's washed up
    Understanding
how ephemeral, and to follow
ephemeral still
    My book goes out before me
to free a space within the world of people
thereby occupying sharks with bait
giving me time to dig in, and
like the surfers say, ride the rail
    There, along the shore everything
even description's breaking
into the mystery of being
    We confuse ourselves
when not involved
with the study of nature

They were wiped out
by winds and waves
and torrent of water's weight
burdening crashing
ceiling and floor
      What if you drop
and descend a fathom
      Wave falling on to the tide
a rushing out to the surf
completely collapsing row of wave
water falling creating suction under water
calm sea today
      Art
the only praxis
a breast all feed upon
      Someone is lost
and it remains to be seen
how long they will be so
      I'd rather root for the underdog
a sweet struggle with or without victory
      People attempt to uncover things all the time

forgetting that it has already been done
within their being
the which's arrogance, deceit's dirigible
   Most, in fact all
people I know
are doing some sort of cover up
with their yakking
   The bedroom's quiet
but for crickets
   Chakras
   We pressure our prejudice to perform
thereby concealing what would otherwise be
added to thought
   How can a fly
have mechanical relation
when what's more, its soul
rots, dies or leaves when man's does
   The coincidences in being
strange spell cast over mind's order
   First thought
most incomplete thought

becoming's brash speculation
  This island's surrounded
the only way out
a hex, crossbar and
something like a motor
  Oxygen
gusting off the ocean
  My model in this and all endeavor
never been any more than that faint
breath of seduction the sweetness of air is
  Those who deny sentience
by way of reason
and reason deny by way of sentient characters
miss the story and truth of man
  Faced with nothing
but work to be done
  Description of a wave
also described a happening
organized within the confines of poetry
  And yet
who wouldn't kill ignorance outright

weave its lessons
into the ground of the sea of man
     People seem not to understand
they are involved with the world
so knock themselves against walls
with relentless glee
     Trying to force myself
to stay in one place
as long as possible
     Another wave-description
to gather all the loose ends
     People love to wield influence
over other people, more so
when it has especially disastrous consequence
     Timing, in the arts
creates a place apart
and that's good
     I have seen wave-roar
from which sight will never
in this lowly creature
able itself with any other bias

Fictions are an organic necessity
telling always the mechanics of materials
whether truly known or not
      Houses
stand on the vanishing shore
      The fear of drowning in being
      The enigma
of the ideogram is sighted
      It's like this
I was born a person
now I must become a man
investigating the nature of being
      Being's a two-backed beast
for sure
      All roads lead to being
which ever was started
in this sense is already finished or found
      You, man, whose entry
made all subsequent journey
magnetize to your first peep
      How many times have I risen

gulped down the myth would
usurp place in head at top of spine
      Becoming a man
one realizes averageness the sameness of selves
the usurpation of one's being
the theft of the letters of one's true name
      What does my experiment
my empiricism
withhold from knowledge, what give
      Recognition's a wave
and pollutes the bloodstream
once and for all time
      Those stairs were once
covered in water, then, subsiding
revealed planks of wood
steps up over dunes onto land
      It's the propinquity
of all these letters, sounds
and significant operations
that bring the furthest into focus
      An overcast morning

and I believe it was raining
a few hours ago
  I see a world of sprites
emerging from the cocoon of my book spun
  The smallest human solicitude
and I'm gushing and weeping
  The inexpressible does not bother
but casts my world
parts half-spoken, join in the groove
reading grove hence a multitude
ferments
  Coupled with weather
the sea can become a ruthless land-eater
  The poor poet looks through the window
at the poor world
  Homonculus come alive
fetish massaged into flight
  They dismiss incompleteness
as failure, and yet fail
in the observation and wisdom
being has with nature

When you tell me to bring the hammer
I feel like spitting out your grave
        To regain the pre-scientific domain
the eye of mankind's machinery
        Sun blinding and becoming eye
in the glistening sand water leaves
        All good poets should try
eliminate sibilance from their song
unless the ocean's their occasion
        Being does not mean
nor did it ever request
the dead
        Ocean's difference water moves
        Acquaintances
never forget, tally invisible ledgers
to snow-plow under
present tense
        Land not watery but below
fire science teaches
        The declaration guts have held from before
calls out always from an omnipresent concern

to find itself in the rabble and confusement
society's obfuscating courtship with disaster
      That jellyfish's now gone
      Nothing is being talked about
but the fact that we can talk
      Suck
and suspension
thunder on a wave's height
      My book broke the sound barrier
so speaks from time's regency
which has many interpretations
among the populace
      Who would deny
the forest of symbol would deny
water's right to feed land
hold abeyant
agricultural man
      But foremost
humanity swallows up
land polluting oceans with
settlements that cover

We can go on dreaming
but the stolidity of ground
and force of the the sea will
still be around
     Spells are cast successfully
because people believe their feelings
dictate their direction, understanding and their
world
     People rarely, I've noticed
bring their placement of things
and relations
up for review or for taste
     Now we have a set theory
where before an organic knee-jerk
un-wed mother and wife held court
     There are characters in this world
searching for themselves
     Nothing bad will happen to man
even his death is not bad, tragic
nor in anyway a loss
     How does this painting function

that is, appearance the only mechanic
hence interpolation twixt concept and percept
defines distant objects of the island
      Not only are the people's minds inconceivable
but right now they're hard at work
      Humans think their being
exclusive of anything else material
immaterial or in potentia
flicker of daylight, sun not bright enough
for the soul of man
      What I call practical
is what I can do
and show by doing it
      To wrangle with a half-heart
no more, letters and vowels teach
      The glitter and trembling
end of a wave, mosaic of what once was
hyaline, majestically predatory
      Any feminist critique
of my letters I predict
will overlook the place in the logos

to which women have assigned themselves
        Responsible
only for my own wanderings
        Blown on a wind or engulfed in a furnace
mind always road-works
sequestered, locked in the releasing earth
        How could anything
be made less present
but by thought, or sense-load
the human vehicle
        The addictive tendencies of methodology
have cast a spell
and fortunately lead us into spell
a gnostic spell whose intimacy
undoes the noxious morality of identity
        Human habitation
leaning out so far unsupported
might one day fall
        How much, or of what do I speak
to bring my relations past
mirrors that contain their mind

From these places
where long time is spent
the scape of its physical reality
remains a mirror for thoughts that occurred there
    I was propelled
because of the forest
        To cast a spell
balance your desires
among certain and uncertain
communicants
        I am writing from inside
all of poetry's assumptions
as a mode of rhetoric and a mode of occupation
identity and its proportion within its own history
        You wait long enough
there's a bi-plane overhead
        I was born into a hyper-egalitarian society
the economics of study
far surpassing other time spent
        Sticking my heels in the sand
        Yet place

presents a praxis
eternal empiricism OR
theory absenting (holding) both
      Literature needs
turn itself away from theatricality
      A small hollow nothing
has phenomena reverberating
land and sea's
      Patterns and pictures
come from the play of presence
and absence
      My release from the public zoo
has only created a private-public zoo
for which I now work
      To stay silent and unspeakable
for as long as you can stand it
then make another ideogram
      We're all under the same spell
      The mosaic
precisely because it is not a method
nor system of signification

belongs to the being of the world
      Now from the rock
a wet rain, and from the ocean
the strophaic mosaic
      I haven't met one person
professes to know
anything but what rumor of mind told
      I am as obscure
and confused
as the public is
      Eternal definition
her hymen's been busted
yet still insists it's intact
      Someone slowly
steps into surf
      I haven't left the water yet
wait
      The ability and abundance of release
women desire and seek out
and find
      Start anywhere, but don't let

those pines needle's
sap infect
     When sea water reaches grass-root
green goes brown
hanging sheaf of dead dune-hair
     What fills with impossible
beating back courage, opting for other
     People who take up the pen
fall first into the assumption
that their own identity must be created
with realizing that this only attracts
a world of identities
whose nature it is to seek out identities
and replace them with them
     I am interfacing with the earth
everything, even the waves seem to stop
mid-motion
     Constant white noise of the ocean
through the top of the windows
     Rhythm reaches
the center of the brain

What mode or sign
controls my move to endeavor
birth to inevitable death
          These the wishes
of a body the body becomes
knows not but what said's happen-would
conventions belief
          Drive me from this shore
and deep, the release from fear
attracts one to the other
          One thing to follow, one thing to write
becoming encounters being
horizon of a real earthscape
          That a woman
can remain unscathed
by the vexations of our age
is incorporated in fact of her willing ease to speak
          To bring the distance near
shine light of becoming in being
          Syntagm is not
and therefore song, through all the world

touches material existence and merges
       History is so often retold
I doubt it has any blood
relevant to our quest for being
       I still feel like someone's child
speak when spoken to, never talk
out of turn, don't raise your voice to me
       I hate the way
and at the point you understand them
they expect some change of behavior
       Were there more to be
here too shows forth
       How can I send it away
if it never leaves
       Lighting a cigarette in the wind
inhaling, and, recalling
a medical textbook's drawing of synapsis
       When will that so relied upon reality
make its presence known, and I enabled
begun again where all assume they've been
       A little yellow bird

atop the dark-berried bushes
around the deck
    When the public encounters mystery
it fobs reality unto
the nearest motion at hand
showing off the beast
    I'm just angry at everyone
for being such an asshole
    Words have meaning
only within the mosaic
    Whole vast legions
cut off from being
my brother saw in San Fran
hiking her skirt, pissing on the street
screaming I'M PISSING ON BABYLON
we both concluded
she should get a life
    Science proves
empiricism's where it is
when epistemology gives way to ontology
    Why do I open,why close

with nothing but the category desire
to hold understanding like a flower holds bee
      The sea wind
makes-over the forest
waving its green
      It's the girlish definitions of the world
that comport me so far out to sea
the sea takes over and rumors me being
      How land and sea merged
is a mystery because they both partake
of mystery
      The blasé comportment
with which disaffected youth
grab and maintain mediocrity
      Knowledge helps no man
it sits in the room's corner
like a television
      Lack of talk in many
social situations means impotence
      Man's vitreous born to die
this world echoes nothing but

With legs spread wide
suspended and on her belly, me
or anyone, plunging that length
       Oh modesty!
close, closer, CLOSER!
       The tympanum's shouts
a barking dog
       Man's world
knows nothing but the face of corruption
yet his nature extends to being
this thought alone
enough for heresy
       Here, in this hour of morning
there's an undulant passage
calm retreating toward low tide
       Those prone to conspiracy-baiting
including Nth generation marxists, socialists
nazis, and patriots
had better take another look around
       Who would worship a tree
undoes theology

to let it rise and transplant
its conduct to the barren moon
        Urging shore-leave
my life's becoming essence
insubstantially dark current
        Two fingers, one almost reaches god
the other almost man
        You thought you could remain neutral
but now there's a spell over you
forcing you to take sides
        I never wanted
to have to think about it
        That understanding
has been taken over by presence
yet remains covered up
        Entrances and exits
posts stuck in sand
I thought were humans
        Have we evolved so far
(or was this much much earlier)
to see what an ignorant state was man

when the simple teacher Jesus
walked upon the land?
      Is there a required
number of skeletons
one has to have in one's closet?
      I can't help but think of Aristotle
every time one of these seagulls
struts before my sitting
      These are my propositions
set forth
      As if it were a dream
I came to myself to discover the self I knew I was
      Being's carried to us on a wave
feeds all other waves to overcome
      That jellyfish looks like a diaphragm
      They pass inspection
here in sand birds cross
      Your task, that is, your life's work
to see into the nature of being
recognizing threads, causes, and just plain
phenomena

To think of man's machines
not as materials nor even operations
but as nodes of principle
    Ownership never forgets
    Never
a choice, but we live
as if at sea, lost and roadless
    All the disguises I've thrown up
as if in desperation
to retrieve my drowning being
    Is it mere bullshit
to assert that the chorus was witnessed
going under the waves?
    I want for nothing more
than my own cadence
    If being's rich, not poorly attired
then where's the man
he a constant hidden factor of existence?
    To overthrow the Cartesian influence
I say goodbye to a world of things
whose confabulations misuse being

and set up a standard for usurious transaction
      Yet am I one
belonging to a great nation
whose space program
my kind and my present mode
help and have helped off the ground
      Bird squabble
unabated, pulsates its shrill wheezing
      Slowly, more water in the waves
get sloppy
      Like a dress-hem retracted
the water's foamy rim

Postface

> Like a dress hem retracted
> the water's foamy rim

The gaze, isolate, clothes the world in memories it seeks to hide,
gaze bury in the world the world the gaze unburies
~~Image~~
~~In~~
Imagine —

It's curtains at the end, see, its curtain's at the sea's edge. And I
imagine: proscenium frame of monumental legs — male female
unclear uncertain unstable. Pale Caucasian calves. Caucasian, lets

not pretend here, ~~now.~~ Whatever the hue. Pale, tall as the columns pretending to hold up — uphold — the courthouse porch, ~~any~~ where, ~~every~~where. Twentyfive-foot calves. See. Ankles the height of second floor windows. And between them, through them, the stage — the sea — extends into the distance forever. The back-wall's the eye's limit, see. That's what they call *upstage.* Stage like a floor of chiseled coal, the sea. One lantern high in the rooftop and a single candle burns on the forehead of the Looker, the Gazer — The Grazer. Here's what you have, I ~~in image~~ imagine —

A single man sits watching the sea at night. He's gazing through these colossus legs, the proscenium arches of the stage. And then, see, I see that all along the beach edge is a line of these huge legs, a protective barrier of gigantic bodies, and, see, they're not all Caucasian, no not nearly not at all. — Like a nonviolence demon-stration against a demonstration of violence, every other colossal body is facing the opposite way — One facing out, *upstage,* the next facing landward, *downstage,* — Back and forth, alternatively, all the way down to the ends of the beach — end of vision — both ways — See, what you have here is a man sitting on a beach, at night, gazing —

The dress hem recedes — *In You I drown* — The curtain goes up,
see, at the end

Reread the <u>Sein und Zeit</u> fragment

Gaze bury in the word the word the gaze unburies

The gaze clothes the word

See, what I had here was a man, sitting at the ocean's edge at night
I glimpse him from a distance, I am up on the dunes, behind him
He can only hear the sea
Its *engine*
I can hear the silence around it
The blood in my ears, that is
I know he hears singing he hears his own singing and it comes to
him in the voices of others
I can see him there, sitting, in the distance
I can hear the silence around him
The blood in his ears, that is

The O, O, O, O of ontology
Tibetan singing bowl
When you hear the voice the invisible is revealed
As hidden

As if from a sentry's tower a searchlight rotates through these pages
— Erratically, like a lighthouse commandeered by pirates — Falls
on specific, vivid stretches of terrain — Holds — Then ripples off
upon the rippled ground — And then the tentspike of the Cogito
is driven into sand — And that is when ~~I in image~~ imagine — The
broken heart's fault begins to vibrate — To sing — Here, see —

> Surprised
> to find my imprint at the beach
> still in place, I could have sat
> all night there and the tide never would've reached

And that is when —
When the Where is fused to the Who — With *Vision* — being
emerges in these pages —
When the cartographer's *Hours* and *Minutes* are unfused —
Then — "suddenly" — hearing the man's thinking I see
his *Where* —
There's a house, poles, a bedroom, birds, a tree + deck, bushes,
deer, — Grazer — jellyfish — But Others? Are there Others? This
seems to be the Call that is being given response to, here, in these
pages —

They say — "When do you hear the call? When you respond." —
Are there Others? Somewhere someone enters the surf. "Who's
there?" There's *Them* and *They* and *You* and *She* and *He* and *It* —
But they are obscured — They are behind glass, they leave prints,
they infuriate, assault, they arouse, they dare, they *subject*, they
shadow — They demand *answer* — *They* <u>memory</u> — They are back
here, with me, *with You*, behind, higher up on the dune, seeing the
man's back as he Faces the waves

> Tired
> the warm but strong sea wind
> easily pushing my eyelids closed

"I know the piece takes place in the daylight as well as the night.
But I am writing this from my memory of the piece as well. And
the night — The chamber — the Site — the Place — Of night —
Is a constant presence in my memory of it. There is a darkness *in*
this light. This seems to be the light of subjectivity. I walk around.
I *see* this. <u>The Corybantes</u> is soaked through with it."

There is a drowning here, a succumbing to subjectivity's *Subjection*
A stinging, hot sun masturbation w/ mirror here
There is a demand, a yearning, to *mean*

There is a hounding, a violence, a flight
There is a contesting, a showing of wounds
  Here, the Words entered, and Here, they left
There is the making of the Book in this book
Accident and memory, universal mosaic law
There is the burying of a Book in this book
"Tod Thilleman"
There is a place
There is a body
Time needs bodies, to pass

To have past

I
~~Image~~
~~In~~

Matthew Seidman Volcofsky
Winterfall '96, Williamsburg, Brooklyn NY

Tod Thilleman is the author of *Wave-Run*, the first in a trilogy of serilogical poems. He is the Editor of *Poetry New York: a journal of poetry & translation*.

Matthew Seidman|Volcofsky (c. 1964-2047)

California, Long Island
Tokyo, New York
$\Big\}$
Wilmington, Delaware

Proprietor, Theater Volkofsky, Roam
Keeping the lamp of darkness lit